The Dominie Collection of Traditional Tales
for Young Readers

Aladdin &
the Magic Lamp

Retold by Alan Trussell-Cullen

Illustrated by Carol Daniel

DOMINIE PRESS

Pearson Learning Group

Once upon a time, there was a boy named Aladdin. His father had died and his poor mother struggled to keep them both fed by sewing clothes for people.

One day a wicked magician rode up to their house on a fine black horse.

"I am your long-lost uncle!" he said to Aladdin.
"I have never heard of any long-lost uncle," said
Aladdin's mother. "What brings you here?"

"I have come to share a great treasure with you," said
the magician. Aladdin's eyes lit up when he heard the
word *treasure.*

"It is hidden in a magical cave," said the magician.
"But I need Aladdin to help me get it."

"I don't like the sound of this magical cave," said
Aladdin's mother. "Make sure you bring the boy back
before nightfall."

The wicked magician rode off with Aladdin. Soon they came to a dark forest. The magician stopped by an old, twisted oak tree. He brushed away some leaves. And there on the ground was a giant ring set in a block of stone.

The magician took hold of the ring and pulled. The stone swung back to reveal a mysterious cave.

"Now it is your turn," said the magician. "Go down into the cave. You will pass through four rooms. In the first three rooms there will be tables covered with precious jewels. You must not touch any of those, for they are magical and will turn you into stone. But in the fourth room, you will find a wooden box. Open the box and you will see an old lamp. Take the lamp out of the box and bring it back to me as fast as you can."

Aladdin made his way through the first three rooms. Precious jewels glittered all around him, but Aladdin remembered the magician's warning. He touched nothing. In the fourth room, he found the wooden box. He lifted the lid and saw the old lamp. He picked it up and quickly ran back to the mouth of the cave.

"Good work, boy!" said the magician. "Pass the lamp up to me and then I will help you climb out of the cave."

Now, Aladdin didn't like the sound of this. "No! I will bring the lamp up with me," he said.

The magician began to get angry. "Give me the lamp right now, you foolish boy!" he shouted.

"No," said Aladdin. "You are trying to trick me! You are not my long-lost uncle at all!"

"If you won't give me the lamp, then you can stay in the cave forever!" the magician screamed.

And he slammed the stone door shut and rode
away at high speed.

Aladdin didn't know what to do. The cave was dark and frightening. "I wonder if this old lamp will give me any light," he said. He rubbed the lamp, and suddenly there was a flash! The cave was flooded with light. A strange figure appeared in front of him.

"I am the genie of the lamp!" the figure said. "Whatever you wish, I will make come true, oh master."

"Well, for a start," said Aladdin, "I wish I were sitting at home right now with my mother."

There was a blinding flash! And the next moment, Aladdin was sitting at home with his mother.

Aladdin told his mother how the wicked magician had tried to trick him, and he tried to explain about the genie of the lamp. His mother nodded her head, but she didn't really believe the story about the lamp.

"Tomorrow we will take the lamp to the market and sell it," she said. "We may get enough money to buy a few beans for our tea."

"A few beans?" said Aladdin. He picked up the lamp and rubbed it with his sleeve. The genie appeared immediately. "Whatever you wish, I will make come true, oh master," the genie said.

Aladdin's mother was stunned.

"Bring us a royal banquet," said Aladdin.

There was a flash, and the next moment their old wooden table was covered with the most amazing feast.

"You see, mother?" said Aladdin. "We could invite the king and his family to join us for dinner."

"Not in these clothes," said his mother.

Aladdin rubbed the lamp again, and the genie appeared. "Bring us some new clothes," said Aladdin. "The best in the land!" Immediately Aladdin and his mother found themselves wearing the most amazing clothes.

"Now we could invite the king and his family to join us for dinner," said Aladdin.

"Not in this old house," said his mother.

Aladdin rubbed the lamp again, and the genie appeared. "Turn this old shack into a magnificent castle!" said Aladdin. There was a flash, and immediately Aladdin and his mother found themselves sitting in a wonderful castle.

"Now we could invite the king and his family to dinner," said Aladdin. And they did.

The King and his family had a wonderful time. In fact, the king's daughter enjoyed herself so much that she fell in love with Aladdin. And thanks to the magic lamp, they soon had a wonderful wedding.